Evangelism through Cells

Reaching out as a cell community

First printed 2003
Reprinted 2004

Cover design by Blue Pig Design Co., Harlow

Published by:
Cell UK Ministries, Highfield Oval, Harpenden, Herts. AL5 4BX

ISBN 1-902144-16-3

Evangelism through Cells

Reaching out as a cell community

Contents

Introduction

This booklet is for everyone involved in small groups whose concern is to love those outside the church with something of the same heart that Jesus demonstrated to us. It is for church leaders, cell supervisors and cell leaders who want to be mobilised as workers in the harvest (Luke 10:2) and want to lead others to become workers too.

It is written specifically for cells which are motivated or want to be motivated from the value of loving the lost. We aim to explain the concept of relational evangelism and to work step by step through a strategy for cell groups as they live out this lifestyle of reaching out to family, friends and workmates through loving friendship.

We want to explore how we can work together in teams to see people experience our loving community and, through that, begin their own journey to accepting Jesus as their Lord and Saviour. When Jesus told His disciples that they would become fishers of men, He was not thinking about angling with a rod and line. He was thinking about fishing nets. Jesus sent out His disciples in fishing teams. What does a modern-day fishing team look like and how should we be living in a way that will see our nets full of fish?

The truth is that we ourselves need this fishing team. We need to be part of a true Christian community which is working together to introduce people to Jesus. This is our cell. The fishing team is there to achieve three things. First, it will hold cell members accountable to love people, which is real friendship. Second, it will seek as a team to build a community which includes all the unchurched friends of the fishing team (the cell) so that our friends see a demonstration of Christian love not just in their one Christian friend but in others. Third, the cell team will work together to see the gospel shared with these friends in a way that will help them to accept Jesus and become disciples within the cell community.

In this booklet we want to give a summary of the evangelism theory and practice that has worked in cell churches, including lessons that have been learnt from several cell churches around the nation. It also includes information about interest groups as a way of developing relationships with unchurched people. We will see that evangelism is about incarnational relationships where we live out and then speak out the gospel to our friends, to our neighbours, to our community, to our workmates.

We are aware that in this booklet we have limited space to develop these concepts. There is further explanation of the underlying philosophy of relationship-based evangelism in *Sowing Reaping Keeping*, and of the new paradigm and impact of post-modernity in *Loving the Lost*, both by Laurence Singlehurst. These books form the foundation for this booklet.

Laurence Singlehurst and Liz West

Confidence in the message

Before we go any further, we need to remind ourselves that we hold the most important message that our world has ever and will ever know. The gospel truly is good news for every family member, friend, neighbour and workmate whom we know.

In our experience we have seen, among Christians, an erosion of confidence in the gospel. We have seen our society move away from one which was largely based on Christian morality, where the Church was an accepted part of the fabric of our communities. We have watched the Church decline in numbers and in influence. We have seen that it has become more acceptable to hold to almost any other set of beliefs than those held by Christians. We realise now that we cannot expect our friends and family to have even a basic knowledge of who God and Jesus are. We have been through a time when many of us have almost lost hope that we will see our friends become Christians. Do we still believe that the gospel is the powerful message which has the ability to save?

> It is time for us to have a new confidence and excitement in the Christian message.

. . . an epidemic of selfishness

Harry Conn, an evangelist of many years ago, said, "You will never get people saved until you get them lost." It has been hard in our materialistic world to identify what 'lost' means. Words such as sin mean very little. But now we are beginning to see what 'lost' actually means. It is a society that is turning away from its base of Christian values. It is individuals who are both the victims and the perpetrators of selfishness. As our moral fabric disappears and people's behaviour becomes increasingly out of control, whether it's a hooligan on the street corner or a well-educated city trader who thinks he can do it his or her way, the government has no real solution. In the past ten years, more laws have been written and changed than in any previous period of history and yet our society becomes more fragmented and increasingly out of control – all signs of an increasing 'lostness'.

What is the answer? Jesus. 2 Corinthians 5:15 says that Christ died for all, that those who live should no longer live for themselves but for Him who died for them and was raised again. This verse shows us that the real power of the gospel is to set us free from ourselves, from the principle of self-rule, from the power of selfishness, because the truth is this: not only are we the victims of selfishness, but also we are selfish.

We can detect that there is a rising recognition in the media and among our friends that we are in trouble, in our community, our nation and even our planet. Here, then is the best opportunity the Church is going to have for years to come. Only Jesus can change people's hearts. The gospel message not only changes hearts, but also gives us a new set of values to live by. Because of God's values, and our respect for people, we live differently. We are no longer promiscuous, we begin to love sacrificially, we have integrity and personal respect.

Sometimes, as we visit churches, we find Christians who love Jesus and would never change from being Christians. This is their personal experience and their story, but deep in their hearts, they are not convinced that their friend or their neighbour needs the gospel or needs Jesus. Reflect on this for a moment. Our society is involved in an epidemic of selfishness. Our whole post-modern way of thinking that says we decide what is right and wrong for ourselves out of our own experience, that we, as consumers, are the ultimate answer to what is right and wrong, and it is a manifesto for rampant selfishness. Is there one of your friends who has not been damaged by someone else's selfishness? Are not marriages breaking down and children being abused because of selfishness? Are not nations at war because of selfishness? What is the answer to this epidemic?

The power of self-centredness will always be difficult to break, but now that our society gives us permission to be selfish, we are making choices dependent on what feels good to 'me' and the whole of our culture is encouraging us to do so. 'If it feels good then do it, or have it . . . and don't think too much about anyone else'. Now we can see that our friends may have everything they want and live for comfort and pleasure, but the results of selfishness are becoming evident. Only opening themselves up to a life lived in obedience to Jesus, empowered by the Holy Spirit, is going to break the rule of self and cause a change in the values that motivate behaviour.

We can have confidence in the gospel because it has an answer for the deepest sickness in our society. Let us not rely on the gospel of comfort where we promise that Jesus will meet all our needs and rescue us from every situation. While this is true in one sense, this message plays straight in to our post-modern view that our comfort and ease should be the central concern. Let us instead preach the gospel of power to break selfishness as we decide to put Jesus first and to make Him Lord of our lives. Let us work together to enable our friends to hear the good news that through Jesus there is a way to break free from the selfishness that can now be seen to be the curse of our families, communities and nations.

Chapter 2

Relational evangelism explained

> Evangelism today has to be driven by relational truth

Change the thinking

Our culture is going through a profound change. As a result, our evangelistic methods need to reflect these changes if we are to make relevant connections with those around us. In much of the Western world we are experiencing a new way of thinking, which requires a new way of going about evangelism. We do not want to criticise what has been done in the past, but just to say that our world is different and we need to approach people in a different way.

A new way of thinking about evangelism

	Old Thinking	New Thinking
1	Truth	Relational truth
2	Decision	Process
3	Winning	Keeping
4	Few	Many
5	Evangelist	Cell

1. Truth to relational truth

Historically, evangelism has been about a truth encounter. "I have the truth, you don't, and you are about to receive it." Either from an evangelist at a meeting, a friend speaking to you, or as you are approached in the street or at your door. It has been about how much of the truth can be conveyed to you. In recent years we have seen that this methodology has become less and less successful. Research by John Finney led us to see that a profound change has taken place. We need to go from truth-based evangelism to relational truth-based evangelism.

Modernity to post-modernity

Our society is going through a huge transition from what we call modernity to post-modernity. At the heart of this there is no longer any overriding truth. There is no one 'story' out there for us to live our lives by. In today's world our own experience rules. Much of the truth-based law that was in our society has been repealed. Now you just behave in any way that feels good to you.
What does this mean to the preaching of the gospel?

Excerpt from *Post-modern Culture and Youth Discipleship*, by Graham Cray
"The most significant dimension of the shift from modernity to post-modernity is the move from a culture in which personal identity and social integration were found through production and the work-place (and thus making a positive contribution to a foreseeable better world) to a culture based on consumption, the market and personal choice now. Even sociologists who resist the term 'post-modern' describe the new shape of society as being centred on consumerism. If this is the case with the overall society it is inevitably central to young people's experience of their world. And it will not do simply to bemoan consumerism as though it could be avoided. We might as well invite fish to live out of the water."

The New Testament gives us a picture of a relational God who is not only telling us the truth, but who also can now be touched, seen and experienced. Hebrews 1:1 says "God has spoken through his son." John writes "The Word became flesh and lived for a while amongst us." (John 1:14). John also writes in 1 John 1:1 "That which was from the beginning, which we have heard, which we have seen with our eyes, which we have looked at and our hands touched – this we proclaim concerning the Word of life." His proclamation was linked to his relationship.

Jesus was a very post-modern evangelist. If He came to a pagan world and demonstrated the gospel by His life as well as speaking about it, we can see that in our increasingly pagan culture we also must live in a way that demonstrates the good news before we can talk about what we know to be the truth. In other words, evangelising in a pagan culture where there is no strong Christian presence requires the gospel to make an impact relationally as well as by content. People around us need to see the effects of the gospel in our lives. They want to see that it makes a difference and they want to experience that difference in us before they will hear our message. John Finney points out that 70 per cent of people who come to faith, do so because they have a Christian friend. (*Finding Faith Today* by John Finney.) See chart – Main factors in journey of faith – on page 12.

Cell-based evangelism is about empowering Christians to make relationships with non-believers.

Our cells are the power-houses to encourage people to be relational.

Main factors in journey of faith

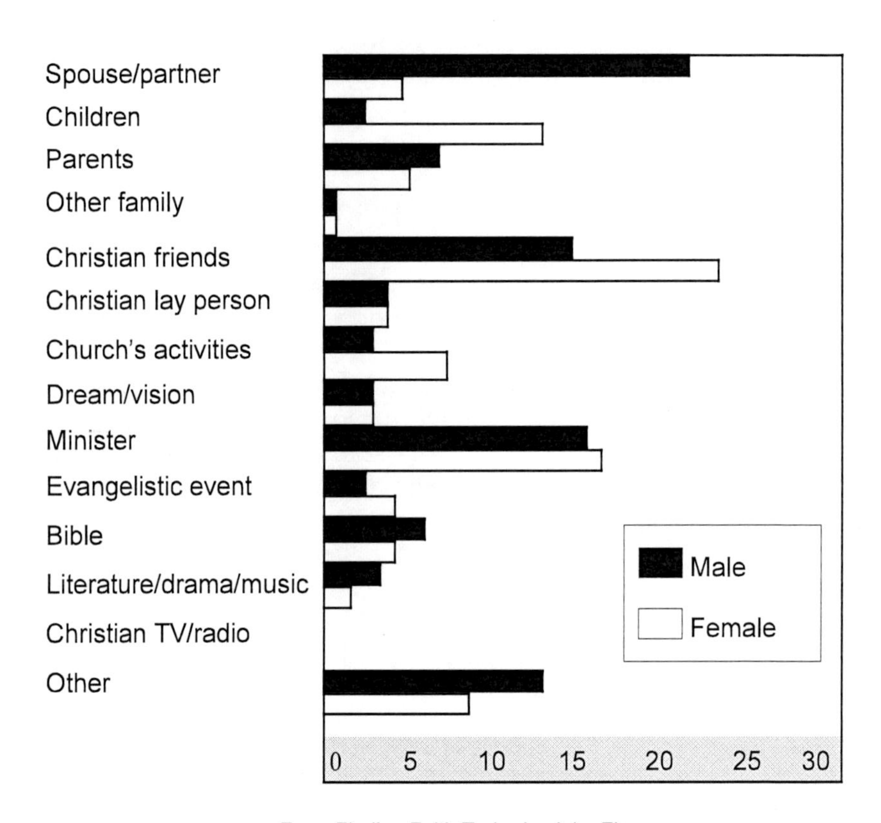

From *Finding Faith Today* by John Finney

2. Decision to process

Understanding evangelism as a process rather than a decision, means that we will be able to effectively engage with non-believers where they are within that process. It liberates us from an old way of thinking where we judged our success by counting the number of heads who had made a decision.

Real evangelism is:

- Identifying where your friend is in the process;
- Through love, words and action, helping them to move up through the process to a decision and on to maturity.

Fruitful evangelism results from:

- Being in relationship with many people;
- Trusting that the Holy Spirit is working in us and through us in this process;
- Believing that through our friendship and our words their minds and spirits are touched so that they begin to have a new understanding of who God is.

Jesus showed us in the parable of the sower (Matthew 13:1-23) that if we make a decision for Christ before we really understand (the rocky soil convert), we will most certainly fall away. The rocky and thorny soil converts have understood the content of the gospel but not the implication. If we are to see real conversion an individual must go through the process of understanding these implications and be honest enough to see where they are personally with regard to this understanding. (See *Sowing Reaping Keeping* for more explanation.)

In real terms, if we ask someone to give their lives to Christ without understanding and relationship, we are asking them to believe in a madman, who could be responsible for all the suffering in the world, and to join the most boring people on the face of the earth, because that's how they see God and how they see us.

If we can build relationship with them and introduce them to a quality Christian community, we will help them to move through the stages on the scale below from a place of suspicion or prejudice against God and Christians, to a decision and on to a life motivated out of the same value system as Jesus demonstrated.

The Engels Scale

-10	Awareness of the supernatural
- 9	No effective knowledge of Christianity
- 8	Initial awareness of Christianity
- 7	Interest in Christianity
- 6	Awareness of basic facts of the gospel
- 5	Grasp implications of the gospel
- 4	Positive attitude to the gospel
- 3	Awareness of personal need
- 2	Challenge and decision to act
- 1	Repentance and faith
0	A disciple is born!
+ 1	Evaluation of decision
+ 2	Initiation into the church
+ 3	Become part of the process of making other disciples
+ 4	Growth in understanding of the faith
+ 5	Growth in Christian character
+ 6	Discovery and use of gifts
+ 7	Christian lifestyle
+ 8	Stewardship of resources
+ 9	Prayer
+10	Openness to others/effective sharing of faith and life

Alpha

This gives us a key as to why Alpha is important. It gives people a relational, non-threatening way to understand the content of the gospel. It engages with them experientially and, also, at several points gives them an opportunity to give their life to Christ.

Alpha is used in all sorts of ways within cell churches. Here is one story that demonstrates how effective it can be to enable multiplication and growth.

"Following an evening discussing how the group was going to move forward, it became obvious that roughly half of the cell had people in their networks that they could invite to Alpha. The other half of the group, while keen on the cell moving forward, did not have friendships with non-Christians sufficiently developed to offer invitations to an Alpha course. It was agreed that the group could multiply around the need to do Alpha with those bringing friends being directly involved and the rest of the group serving in the evangelism process by meeting to pray and cook meals in the opening weeks.

The course duly kicked off with a supper party and introduction to the material with the invited friends sat around in the lounge; it all seemed very encouraging. Two married couples, a young lad in his early 20s, another man slightly older, and a young mum, made up the guests on that first evening. The group met in different cell members' homes over the following weeks and meals duly arrived from the other half of the group. The teaching discussion was all done together as the group was small enough not to need to split up. An interactive teaching style was used that encouraged questions and discussion through the evening. This often involved the cell members sharing their own experiences and not always the speaker giving the answers. The evening always started with a meal, followed by coffee and an ice-breaker which was linked to the topic for the evening.

It was great to see the community form over the opening weeks. On week five one of the couples on the course suggested a meeting at their house and the other couple offered to bring the meal. This showed the level of ownership in the group.

We had planned to go away for the Holy Spirit weekend but this proved a real challenge with various commitments and children to be looked after. So we spent Saturday together doing the sessions at one of the couple's homes and got pizza and watched football that evening. We gathered again for Sunday morning and for the final 'How can I be filled?' session and shared a very special time where those present made commitments to God.

To encourage the development of relationships in the group and discipleship of those who had come to faith they were paired up with cell members to begin the one-on-one discipleship material using Ralph Neighbour's New Believers Station *and* The Arrival Kit.

The group finished the Alpha sessions over the ensuing weeks and were so excited by the experience that they wanted to invite friends, relatives and work colleagues. Following a short break of around three weeks a second course was started. To allow the initial group to continue, Alpha was run fortnightly and met as a cell on alternate weeks. For this second course the cell leaders and existing Christians in the group were encouraged to do some of the talks. They were well prepared and supported during the evenings and afterwards, if required. Following the second Alpha course the new people were added in and the cell has continued. Eighteen months on it is just about to multiply again through running a marriage course as a means to fold in new people."

3. Winning to keeping

In the days when local church was seen as a normal part of everyone's experience, the emphasis was on winning people to Christ. They could become Christians and find their place in church life. Today we need to think about keeping them. If we want to see them become disciples who live the Jesus lifestyle in our pagan world, we need to build our strategies based on that idea. We probably need to ask some questions about ourselves and ask if anybody would like to join us. Are we easy people to be friends with, do we really care, do we really love? We may have to re-adjust accordingly, learn some new relational skills and be prepared to be flexible in the way we go about our lives together.

4. Few to many

In the old way of thinking, evangelism was something that was done by the few. Now in cells everyone gets involved in evangelism. We will never reach the lost through the anointed ministry of a few people. Loving the lost is an obligation upon us all. We are all needed in this ministry of building quality relationships in this culture where relationship is so important. Whether we are five years old or 85, we can have non-Christian friends and we trust that the dynamics of our life and our behaviour will make an impact on them. We can ask the Holy Spirit to influence them and help them to change their minds about God.

5. Evangelist to cell

The old paradigm was held up by the evangelist. Church strategies were built around evangelists and missions. They came and equipped us for these events. We worked to bring friends to hear their message. The cell holds up the new paradigm where evangelism and loving people is all the same thing, and we are being empowered by our cell to build true community. On a week-to-week basis we are challenging each other to reach out, recognising the dangerous time is when we as Christians become insular and isolated. We could become the most holy and spiritual group of people around and be no threat to the powers of darkness, providing the only people we know are Christians and we stay locked up in our buildings, our meetings and even our homes.

The challenge for cells

The challenge that we want to give ourselves is to each have three local friends. These are people we are reaching out to because God has put love in our hearts and we want to express love to them.

> To have three friends you might need to know 20 acquaintances.

The real cell community is made up of the Christians and their non-Christian friends.

A Cell Community

The inner circle: the cell members meeting together on a regular basis

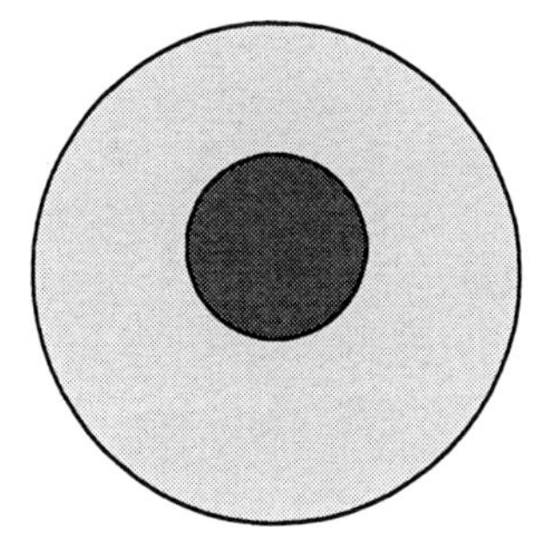

The outer ring: The cell members' network of non-Christian relationships

Even though these non-Christians might not come to our cell meeting, they need to be seen as part of the cell community. Cell-based evangelism is NOT bringing non-Christians to the cell, but rather empowering Christians into relationships. However our friends come to faith, through Alpha or other church-based activities, they will have already experienced being part of the cell community, which will enable them to then come into the cell meeting.

Cell-based evangelism is NOT bringing non-Christians to the cell, but rather empowering Christians into relationships. It is 'GO' rather than 'COME' evangelism.

Starting an epidemic

We can learn from the understanding of how disease is spread. Epidemiologists ask five questions when they try to evaluate how serious a disease will be:

1 How serious is the disease? This addresses the ultimate consequence of the disease. Is it the inconvenience of a common cold or the a life-threatening disease such as Aids or cancer?
2 How contagious is the disease? This is about the transmission of the disease. How easy is it to catch? Is it passed on by a sneeze or sharing body fluid?
3 How long will the person be infected? The duration of the infection determines how many others will be infected. Will the infection period hang on for a long time and thus increase the number of people infected?
4 How infected is the person with the disease? Does the individual have a mild case? Does the person have a virulent dose of the disease?
5 How many people come into contact with the disease? This is about exposure. How many people are in danger of being exposed to the disease?

From Redefining Revival, by William A. Beckham

Spread the disease of Christianity

The pressure on Christians is to know only Christians and to be so busy in our church programmes that we have no capacity for more relationships. We are no threat to Satan's kingdom. The lost are never going to see something of the love of Christ through us. It is the purpose of cell-based evangelism to start a mighty epidemic for Jesus. In your cell you are affected by the love of Christ and you are empowered to share that love with as many people as possible. Loving people is going to be tough. On occasion it will require us to love others enough to lay down our own desires for their sake. I don't know about you, but I need all the love and encouragement and accountability to keep going.

Do you have a contagious dose of the disease in the first place?	If our non-Christian friends spend time with us, what chance do they have of catching Christianity?	Every non-Christian who meets us meets with Jesus so that they are changed by the encounter in their attitudes.
How contagious is the disease?	How easily does Christianity spread in our nation?	Only by prayer and on-going contact with the life of Christ lived out in an attractive Christian community will Christianity be other than ridiculed in our nation.
How many people do you know?	How many non-Christians do we know?	An isolation hospital contains infectious diseases.

Questions:

1 What gives you your confidence in the gospel?
2 Why is speaking the truth not as effective as it once was?
3 How are relationships important in conveying the gospel?
4 Describe the process that a non-Christian has to go through before they can fully understand what it means to be a Christian.
5 What do you think they need to understand?
6 What hinders your friends from giving their lives to Christ?

Chapter 3

Building a network

Expressing love by building friendships

As God has expressed His love to us, so we are called to express love to others. We are called as Christians to be witnesses (Acts 1:8), to talk about our experiences, and our story of God, with those who don't yet know Him. In doing this we are taking the risk of sharing our greatest treasure with friends, family and work colleagues who might not be interested. This witness is about the love that we have for those who are described as 'lost'. It is not about building friendships in order to see people converted. It is about loving people so much that we want to build a relationship with them which will give us the opportunity to share our greatest treasure with them.

As we think about the practical dynamics of building relationships, so forming a network of unchurched friends, what we are really talking about is 'loving people'. We often need help and encouragement to do this.

> 'Hospitality' the secret ingredient in relational evangelism in the 21st century.

How are we going to go about becoming relational and hospitable?

One of the important things to understand about friendship in our present culture is that all friendships are made in the context of something else. Being friendly to strangers on the streets of your local town is not the context in which friendships are made. But if you get involved in the infrastructure of society and become part of the normal social scene, you earn the right to share names with one another, just by being in a common context with people. You make an acquaintance and out of that acquaintance comes the possibility of a friendship.

Building a network of relationships

At church meetings
People come to our churches for all sorts of reasons. Some of them are unchurched and there is a wonderful opportunity through our Sunday meetings to be friendly, to reach out with practical love to show that our interest in people is real. We all need to take on the responsibility of being aware of new faces and to be ready to lay another place for Sunday lunch.

Through social action and caring projects
Many of our churches are looking for volunteers who can serve in social action programmes, whether it be a mums and toddlers group, a counselling service, a homeless outreach, or some other practical social action programme. As we volunteer and reach out through that programme, we will undoubtedly meet people and have an opportunity to be a friend. Someone who starts off as an acquaintance may then develop into something more.

Through our social network
In all our communities, there are opportunities for positive citizenship where we can take our Christian values and our love into the infrastructure of our community. We can join a political society, join a parent/teacher association, neighbourhood watch, or one of the many other committees and organisations that make up our local communities.

Through leisure activities
Building friendship from acquaintance takes time and energy. We recognise that as Christians we should love in a sacrificial way, but the fact is that making friendships with non-Christians does not have to be a chore. We can meet new people and develop relationships with them through the activities that we enjoy doing anyway. We will find that we already have things in common and a context in which to meet.

So ask yourself, what do you enjoy doing? Is it golf? Is it walking? Is it arts and drama? Anything you enjoy, providing it doesn't contravene God's value system. Then all we need to do is find opportunities to do this activity in a context where there are non-Christians. We will find that we do have energy for it. For example, my friend Jeremy plays golf every week with two friends. Jane is a member of a mums and toddlers group. Tim is in the running club. Paul plays snooker and so on.

At work

As Christians, we take our value system to work and work hard, with integrity. We have a mandate to be salt and light and make an impact on our society by our value system. One hundred years ago people worked where they lived and because of that it was known that they went to the church or chapel. This was a major factor in church growth. Today we live within a different sociological frame-work. Most of us do not work where we live, and even if we work where we live, the people we work with don't live where they work. Our work relationships continue to be important evangelistically, but they will not help our local churches to grow. If your work colleague begins to explore Christianity with you, they may find it difficult to relate to Christians where they live because they have no context for relationship with them. Your responsibility will be to journey with them within the work context.

Rebuild our local communities

An important factor in the revivals of 100 years ago was that every-body knew everyone else because they lived and worked in the same community. Here is a challenge for us. Can we rebuild local community through our networks of friendships? Through our good works and love, through our words and witness, will people see and experience and hear the dynamic of this wonderful gospel?

The challenge that we want to place before each one of us is that we are called to love people and build friendships. Rebuilding community is a very practical way of loving people. It so happens that this is also the most effective way of people seeing a living demonstration of Christianity which becomes a platform for the

Holy Spirit to reveal Jesus to them. Slowly but surely they become open to hearing the words and experiencing more of the wonders of the Christian gospel. Can each of us develop friendship with, say, three non-Christian acquaintances and can we support each other in our cells to make this a reality?

- A friend is one joined to another in intimacy and mutual benevolence apart from sexual or family love.
- An acquaintance is someone whom you are made aware of or familiar with, more than mere recognition and less than intimacy.

Turning acquaintances into friends

Those of us who have been Christians for a period of time might well have only Christian friends. The challenge is to make contact with non-Christians and then turn those acquaintances into friendship. Our motivation will be to love these people, to get to know and understand them so that we can demonstrate acceptance and be ready to serve them when they have needs.

Pray for them on a daily basis;
Spend time with them as often as possible. Find a context in which to do that;
Listen to them and show them respect in doing so;
Ask questions and show them you care by being interested in them;
Be hospitable. Invite them to your home, which is your greatest asset in friend building;
Risk honesty at the right time and in an appropriate way share yourself with them;
Serve their needs as they express them to you, in practical ways;
Introduce them to your Christian friends so they can experience a community of honest, accepting, trusting love.

Witness idea:
If you are at the stage in your cell where you are wanting to encourage your members to develop their relationships from acquaintance to friendship you could try using the following idea in the Witness section of the meeting.

Discuss the difference between a friend and an acquaintance and ask each member of the group to identify a couple of friends and a couple of acquaintances who are not Christians.
In pairs, ask them to discuss how they can develop relationships with these acquaintances. Ask them to be specific about the next step and hold each other accountable to do whatever they have discussed. This will need to be followed up regularly in the cell to encourage the on-going development of relationship.

Sowers and reapers

By nature and by experience some of us are better at building friendships than others. We are more natural sowers. We are naturally good at building friendships. Some of us are probably better at speaking about the realities of the Christian life and are more natural reapers. In any cell, it is probable that some will have a large network of relationships and others a very small one. We are learning within our cells to work together as a team. By building one another into our circle of relationships we are evangelising by the means of a net, rather than on an individual line and rod basis. We each contribute from our strengths, gifts and experience. We are creating a fishing team and we learn to love people together.

Use the following questions in your group to start a discussion to help people discover if they are more likely to sow, reap or keep.

Sowers enjoy making non-Christian contacts. Who has lots of non-Christian friends and how do they make them?

Reapers like to share the content of the gospel with people and find it easy to share their testimony and invite people to Christian events where the gospel will be preached. Who enjoys doing this in the group?

Keepers are concerned with what will happen as people come to faith and who will be responsible for their growth in the faith. Who in the group identifies with this area?

Friend-making becomes a lifestyle

If we are going to discover the great joy of making friends with those outside the Church we will probably need to make a change in our lifestyles. There will be some hard choices about how we spend our time. We will only see fruit in our relationships if we invest more of ourselves, particularly our time and our prayers, into building deeper friendships. We want our friends to experience high quality love, the love that can only come as we give to them out of the love that we have received from our Heavenly Father. It will involve taking a risk on our part.

Friend-making will require our churches to be less demanding of our time. We will need to be freed from so many meetings to give us time to work with our cell community to reach out to those outside the Church. It will need to become more of a priority. We will need energy and creativity as we seek to develop our cell community to include the three friends of each cell member.

Let's ask ourselves some questions:

1 What have I learnt in this chapter?
2 What is an effective way to love people in our modern culture?
3 What is the difference between an acquaintance and a friend?
4 List the people with whom you spend more than one hour a month, whose both Christian name and surname you know and who live in your area. These are people who might become your friends.
5 How can you make friends? What context could you join to build a network?
6 What is a natural way for you to love people? How can you develop that to operate in the context of friendship?

Chapter 4

Eight steps to implementation

Introduction

In this chapter we want to put the theory of chapters one, two and three into action. The purpose of these eight steps is to change the beliefs and values and, consequently, the actions, of your individual cell members and collectively their cell groups. We hope that in following these steps, individuals and cell teams will develop a heart for loving others and reaching out to them with the wonder of the Christian gospel.

This is a tried and tested strategic plan for cell evangelism, but it will need to be adapted for each cell. We will make some suggestions as to how the Witness section of a cell meeting can be used as the strategy develops. We believe that without some such plan, cells will not be effective in seeing people become Christians. It takes hard and persistent work for a group to become an effective fishing team.

Step 1 - Change the value
Step 2 - Prayer
Step 3 - Accountability
Step 4 - Rebuild community
Step 5 - Develop an interest group
Step 6 - Content of the gospel
Step 7 - Create opportunities for your friends to become Christians
Step 8 - Growing the cell group with new Christians

A couple of warnings

Warning number one
Many cells are in the habit of asking different cell members to lead

different sections of the meeting. This encourages every member to contribute and is to be commended. However, when the Witness section is delegated in this way the forward movement of the cell towards reaching the lost can be affected. In fact the witness of the cell often swerves to praying week by week rather than to 'prayer-supported evangelistic activity'. The cell members become discouraged and the cell never sees anyone come to faith. It is our recommendation that one person takes responsibility for leading the Witness part of the cell meeting. If there is an evangelist in the group he or she could take on this responsibility. If not, then maybe the cell leader needs to lead the Witness section and thereby keep the cell moving in its mandate to reach the lost and multiply.

Warning number two
It is the sad story of many cells that the Witness section frequently gets left out as the Welcome, Worship and Word expand to fill the time. These groups become inwardly focused, more like house groups than cells. Keeping the momentum of the outward focus requires disciplined time management through the meeting. It can be helped by changing the order of the 4Ws so that the Witness comes before the Word. Our witness as a cell should be the climax of our activity together – it is, after all, the reason why the Church exists, to reach the lost and to make disciples. In a cell which has the value of loving the lost, this time-keeping issue is not such a problem as the group is motivated to make friends and to see them become Christians. If this value is not in place then the leaders need to be ever alert to keeping the outward focus on a weekly basis and to keep planning activities which include non-Christians.

STEP 1 Change the value

Goal: to approach evangelism, not motivated by guilt or legalism, but by a true understanding of Christ's love for the lost and His commitment to them. From this understanding grows a desire to be obedient to Jesus and to love our 'neighbours' as He did, consistently and sacrificially, not counting the cost.

Check the scriptures:

Luke 19:10	Jesus said that He came to seek and save the lost.
2 Corinthians 5:14	Christ died for all.
John 3:16	God so loved the world.

We can conclude that God loves people. They are made in His image, His heart is broken by them. God, through Christ, wants to reach out to people and enable them to come back to a wonder of wholeness and relationship with Him.

Where do we start? With our motivation.
Why do we reach out to people in the first place? Is it because we want more people in our church? More bottoms on the seats? The answer to this should be 'no'.

If we are disciples of Jesus we will be motivated to reach out to people as Jesus did. Our motivation will stem not from 'ought' – a legalistic bind over us – but from a desire to love people as Jesus did. Our friends, neighbours, family and work colleagues need to know that they have value. They need to know that they are not whole without a restored relationship with God their Father and a life motivated not for themselves, but in living for Christ. The reality is that many of us who have been Christians for some time come to Jesus' command to love the lost carrying our own baggage from past experiences. Often we have painful memories of rejection, or being told to do things that have not sat easily with us. We have possibly been discouraged by a lack of response.

In Step 1 the cell has an opportunity to work through these issues, pray for healing and create a new understanding about relational evangelism and our need to be obedient in loving our neighbour. This is foundational and should take as long as the group needs to take to undo wrong thinking and hurtful past experience. When a Christian has the value of loving the lost as Jesus does, they will be prepared to try again. They will understand what they have to offer, how they can demonstrate love. They will see the need for some lifestyle changes in order to free time for relationships with people outside the Church. They will see the need for strategy as the group plans together how they will reach out.

Step 1 Witness outlines

Witness 1

Read Jesus' mission statements in Luke 4:18-19 and Luke 19:10. Go around the group and ask each member to say how they have benefited as a result of Jesus' mission. They can share how they became Christians or how they have been healed or set free. End with a prayer thanking the Lord for His work in our lives and asking to be used by Him to reach others.

Witness 2

Ask the questions:
When you look at people who don't know Jesus, what do you see? You are looking for answers such as: they seem fine without God; they have everything they want – more than I do; it seems impossible that they would ever show any interest in God; I feel threatened by them as they seem so 'all together'; they are lost and don't know it; they need to be loved.
Record these answers on a large sheet of paper laid out on the floor in the centre of the group. Divide the sheet into two columns recording these answers on one half. Then ask:
How do you think Jesus sees them? (Unbelievers are called sheep without a shepherd, lost, poor, prisoners, blind.)
Record these answers on the other half so that the group can see where there is a difference in the way they see non-Christians and how Jesus sees them.
Pray for one another to see non-believers as Jesus does and for Him to show you something of the love that He has for people, that you may be motivated out of that love.

Witness 3

We are asked (implied) by Jesus to be workers in the harvest field (Luke 10:2) and to go and make disciples (Matt 28:18-20). Read these verses and ask the group: What motivates you to reach out to the lost (guilt or love)? Give a few minutes of silence for reflection before each person answers. Encourage honesty by answering first and including your own struggles. Pray for each other for healing of past hurts and rejection from non-believers or from past church situations where they have felt uncomfortable or even abused when it has come to previous evangelistic endeavours. This may take more than one cell meeting. The important thing is to persevere in ministry until there is a sense of individuals experiencing release.

Witness 4

In Chapter 1 we described relational evangelism.
Ask your cell to define relational-based evangelism. Create a definition on a sheet of paper to prevent this discussion becoming too open ended.
How can truth be carried in the context of relationships?
Pray for God to inspire and anoint the relational skills and opportunities of all the cell members.

Witness 5

Remind the group of the definition of relational evangelism which you created together last time.
How does hospitality become a key in this new evangelism?
Ask the group to share accounts of their experiences of using their homes in building relationships with non-believers.
Pray for one another in this area of hospitality. Where are the difficulties that need to be overcome? Pray for the Lord to bless the plans you have in place already to use your homes to build relationships.

Witness 6

Ask the group:
How has our motivation to become witnesses changed over these past weeks?
We should be motivated out of love and compassion for those who are described as lost. We should also be motivated by our love for Jesus which works itself out in obedience (John 14:15).
If there are still problems, ask for honesty and pray for these individuals. Be prepared to work with individuals outside the cell meeting to help them prepare to become part of the fishing team.

STEP 2 Prayer

Goal: to develop a lifestyle of prayer for the world around us on two levels: for individuals and for our country and community. Through prayer we learn to take responsibility for each others' friends.

Part of the process of changing our values is to agree with God that His view of our neighbourhood and our friends is the correct view. As we pray we begin to take on godly values and mindset – we are changed. We need to pray personally and corporately to this end.

This prayer will need to be persistent, particularly with the spiritual climate in which we live where few people seem to be seeking our God and where knowledge of Him is increasingly limited. In the battle to develop a consistent prayer life it is helpful to be accountable to others in our cells. If we set prayer targets which are specific then we are more likely to get on with the task of praying for our non-believing friends and contacts. We can also set aside time each week to pray in our cell meetings for the communities around us and the individuals with whom we are in contact.

An important aspect of cell evangelism is working together as a team. It is essential that we learn to take responsibility for each others' friends and family. This responsibility develops as we pray for each others' friends even before we have met them. Having prayed consistently for them, when we do meet them we feel a different bond with them. They experience our love and concern without really knowing us. It can completely amaze them! Although Step 2 is entitled Prayer, praying for individuals and activities needs to be a regular and ongoing part of cell life. Some cells will call a half-night of prayer for their outreach every two or three months instead of running a 4Ws meeting. This can be a special time of fellowship over a shared meal and then a longer period of grappling in prayer for non-believing friends and family.

Step 2 Witness outlines

Create witness outlines from the following ideas:

Praying for our communities: Pray big-picture prayers

Declaration

- declare over our town and over our friends, that each individual is important and loved by God.

Intercession

- ask God for the fullness of everybody's potential to be released, for His blessing on our communities.
- ask that people would begin to see God for who He really is and to see that His Church and His people are okay.
- ask God to establish His kingdom on our patch, our neighbour-hood or workplace. Ask Him to overcome Satan's activity in our sphere of influence.

> Action: Walk around your neighbourhood and pray for God's kingdom to come.

Think
What is it that keeps my friends in this village, town, or city from knowing Christ? We could pray to break the power of these things so that they would not hold back our friends. For example:

- Materialism and hedonism. The wonder of things, the pursuing of pleasure and the avoidance of pain is the number one occupation of most people in our culture. This insulates them from pain and difficulty and from having a sense of being lost.
- Apathy. A sense that life is only important in the present and a lack of interest in bigger things and finer things.
- A negative picture of the Church. There is no doubt that most people have either subconsciously or consciously felt the impact of a certain picture of us as Christians and of the message of the gospel. It might be through television dramas where Christians are portrayed as hypocrites. Or they may have had, for whatever reason, a genuinely difficult or unhappy experience with a church or a Christian.
- Fear. All sorts of fears hold people back; fear of commitment, of change, of their circumstances, fear of looking foolish.

Praying for workers in the harvest

Jesus didn't ask the disciples to pray for the harvest. He said that was already there. What He wanted was more workers to go into the harvest (Luke 10:2). We need to pray specifically and consistently for ourselves as we commit to working in the harvest. Pray regularly for cell members as they meet with friends, family and colleagues so that they become effective workers.

Praying FOR individuals: Pray small-picture prayers

It seems extraordinary that God has chosen us to be fellow workers with Him in seeing our friends become Christians. We can be a part of seeing those whom we care about having the opportunity to choose a relationship with Jesus through the prayers that we pray for them.

We can pray for:

- God to bless our friends. Know them well enough to know their immediate needs. He answers prayers for non-believers because He loves them and wants them to come to know Him.
- Specific friends to become Christians. Take up the challenge of developing friendships with three people who don't yet know Jesus.
- God to bless our relationships with friends and for wisdom to know how to develop these friendships.
- Opportunities to speak about our beliefs.
- Opportunities to introduce our friends to the cell community.

Praying WITH non-Christians

It is a constant challenge to build relationships with friends to the point where they are sharing their needs. It can be an even greater challenge to dare to offer to pray with them, there and then, when they are sharing their difficulties. It is an exciting adventure to pray with non-believers if they will let you. People are generally very open to this. It enables God to show them how much He loves them and when He does answer prayers for them there can be no denying that something has happened as a result of prayer. This can be such a significant moment for someone who may not even be seeking God.
Learn how to offer to pray for a friend in a way that will not cause them embarrassment, by discussing how to do this in a Witness section. You could even role play these situations so the group gains in courage. Hold one another accountable to take up opportunities as they arise.
Pray for God's blessing on your outreach activities as a group.
As the cell begins to work together in outreach, every step needs to be covered in prayer. We would go so far as to say that unless the cell is praying there will be no fruit from their endeavours.

STEP 3 Accountability

Goal: to hold each other accountable to becoming 'workers in the harvest' (Luke 10:2).

Why do we need to be accountable to one another? We all know that we believe certain things but we never actually do them. For example, we can believe that we love Jesus and want to be obedient to Him, but we get involved in the reality of everyday life only to discover that our best intentions get lost along the way. We know certain things are true, but for all sorts of reasons we don't follow that belief into action. To believe the right things is easy. To do the right things can be hard. We all need help to obey the commands of Christ. It is a real challenge for us to love the lost as Jesus has asked us to in a practical and effective way (Matt 22:39). We need encouragement from others to keep going. It is helpful if we recognise our tendency to put things off or not get around to doing what we said or thought we would do.
Paul had the same problem which he described in Romans 7:14-20. He recognised that he didn't naturally do what he ought to do. We are the same and need each other to help us and hold us accountable. Perhaps it is in this area of loving the lost that we need the most encouragement from each other.

Step 3 Witness outlines

Witness 1

As a cell, give each other permission to hold one another accountable to:

- the value: do we really see people the way God sees them?

Question: Jesus was the friend of sinners. Am I? What have I done which demonstrates that I am loving the lost?

Be gentle with your cell members, but encourage them to be honest about how they are really doing. Pray for each other to make the next move forward. Their next steps can be small and need to be achievable so that they are encouraged to keep going. It is good to celebrate these steps as they move forward.

Witness 2

As a cell, give each other permission to hold one another accountable to:

- love people by building relationships with them, by being their friends.

Question: Am I building a network of friendships?
All friendships are made in the context of something else. Ask your cell members to develop their own strategy for building their network.
What am I doing or would like to do in my local area?
How am I or can I be involved in my area?
Which club do I belong to or could I join?.
How am I using my home to develop my network of friends?
Work towards each member being able to complete the following statement so that they can be held accountable by the cell for developing their own network of friends:

I will get involved in ....
so that I can love people.

Witness 3

As a cell, give each other permission to hold one another accountable to:

- use their gifts to reach the lost.

Make a list together of all the things that your cell members enjoy doing and have the gifts to do. Include the spiritual as well as practical gifts. Begin to get people thinking as to how they can use these gifts to see people become Christians.

Evangelism styles taken from Bill Hybels' book
Become a Contagious Christian Published by Zondervan

Confrontational	*Intellectual*	*Testimonial*
♦ Confident ♦ Assertive ♦ direct	♦ Inquisitive ♦ Analytical ♦ logical	♦ Clear communicator ♦ Story teller ♦ Good listener
Interpersonal	***Invitational***	***Serving***
♦ Warm personality ♦ Conversational ♦ Friendship orien-tated	♦ Hospitable ♦ Relational ♦ Persuasive	♦ Others centred ♦ Humble ♦ Patient

STEP 4 Rebuild community

Goal: to develop a community which includes your cell's non-Christian friends.

Check the Bible; John 13:35 says, "All men will know that you are my disciples if you love one another."

It has been observed that nearly every spiritual awakening in history, every revival, has broken out in communities with two sociological factors: people work where they live, and everybody knows everybody. While we cannot change the first of these two factors, we can do something about the second. There was a time when you would have known most of the people in your block of flats or in your street.

If we are going to touch our nation, we as the Church must set about rebuilding community. The vision behind cell church is to rebuild community so that every cell is like two circles, one inside the other. The inner circle is the cell meeting and the relationships between the Christians, and the outer circle is the relationships those Christians have within their area. See page 17. This is, if you like, the real cell. Some members of your real cell, in fact most members, may not be Christians and never come to the cell meeting, but you have embraced them into your community. As a result you are not just reaching these people on your own, fishing as it were with a rod, but you are loving them corporately, creating, as it were, a net. So through social events, through practical help, fun, and parties, you are getting to know each others' non-Christian friends and your non-Christian friends are getting to know other non-Christians who are the friends of other Christians in your cell. In reality the more that cell members have in common, the more able they will be to create this community. If your cell is made up of men who like football, the outreach strategy becomes obvious and the focus of the community is around its main interest. When cells are made up of a broad mix of people it can be more difficult to create this wider cell community. In some cases it might be necessary to re-configure the cells around an outreach focus. In other cells, a subgroup of the cell can work together to reach a particular group. For example two couples in the cell can run a marriage course for non-Christians, supported by the rest of the cell, who might offer to baby-sit, provide food and pray for the course.

This phase of the outreach strategy of a cell can take many months of patiently building the community, especially if cell members begin with very few real relationships with non-Christians in their neighbourhoods. It is a very important phase and worth giving time and effort to it. The result can be that you have permission to talk about the gospel with many non-believers who would otherwise have been closed to your message. It needs to be a fun time and can be very exciting as you see friends warm up to the first Christian community they have come across.

An honest moment

While building the wider community, an opportunity is created to help those cell members who struggle with their inter-personal skills. Not all Christians are a good advertisement for Jesus. Their past experiences may have left them unable to relate to others.

They might be unable to reach out to others, or perhaps have quirky mannerisms that do not encourage outsiders to want to stick around. The challenge for the cell is to become honest enough with each other that it is possible to talk about these difficult things. It is for the sake of the lost, but it could also revolutionise the lives of these individuals who might have been secretly longing to be able to make better relationships.

Step 4 Witness outlines

Witness 1

For fun, offer a prize in your cell for whichever member knows the Christian names and surnames of the most people in their street or block of flats.

Question: What could we do as a cell that would help build this community? Plan with your cell how to build a corporate community.

- Celebrate birthdays and invite your friends as well as cell members to the party.
- Using your inner and outer community, organise a charitable event which gets everybody doing something together.
- Get the cell working together to help a non-Christian friend in a practical way – move house, decorate, do some gardening.
- Arrange social events to which you can invite both the inner and outer communities.

Witness 2

What contributions can your cell members make to building the cell community?
Many people can be daunted by the prospect of evangelism, but can arrange a social event, send out invitations, prepare the venue, cook food, chat to people as they arrive, pray for the event, and so on. Ask your cell members which gifts they have which will enable them to contribute towards an event, so that everyone can be involved and enjoy making their contribution.

Witness 3

As you plan a social event, pray that the love of God would permeate all that you do.

Witness 4

Situations may arise in people's lives where they have some kind of practical need. Take this as an opportunity to reach out and plan how the cell will meet their need. If a more profound need arises, some kind of illness, financial difficulty, some kind of breakdown, then you and your cell reach out and care. Pray for God to use this as a time when these friends will become more open to your message.

Witness 5

Discuss how each cell member can increase their contact time with each of their non-believing friends. What would be a realistic goal for each relationship? How could this goal be reached – or what do we each have to plan in order to spend more quality time with our friends? Commit your plans to the Lord and hold each other accountable for them.

STEP 5 Develop an interest group

Goal: to enable the cell to work out how they can increase contact with non-Christians by sharing with them their skills and abilities.

What is an interest group? This is an idea developed by Ralph Neighbour, but in practice it has been happening without a name for many years. It is where you as an individual Christian, working with others from your cell, bring together a number of non-Christian friends around a mutual interest and form a social group around that interest that lasts for a limited period of time. The goal is that somewhere through that shared activity you will not only build a greater sense of community but also the people attending will see an attractive example of true Christian community. They will become more open to your message when they have tasted the experience of an open, loving community.

In my cell, one of the members has a lot of friends, other young fathers like himself. He has run two interest groups. The first one met for five or six sessions, on a fortnightly basis, around the idea of fathers and sons, talking about how they could be better fathers. The fathers gathered, chatted, and eventually went away for a weekend with their sons. In one of those sessions they looked at some of the Christian principles and values which help men to be better fathers. They also looked at a number of secular principles that were applicable to everyone.

A year later, the same cell member did another interest group built around the effect of post-modernity on work and family. Again four or five non-Christians turned up on these evenings, and mingled with the cell members, which strengthened relationships.

However it is organised, an interest group gives an opportunity to deepen relationships because of the increased contact. Often, if it is discussion-based, someone might be able to witness to what

God has meant to them in the circumstances under discussion. This may lead to more general discussion about faith, or create opportunities for individual conversations at other times. It is a significant step on the journey for many non-believers who though not actively seeking God, become intrigued by meeting real Christians who are seeking to live out their faith in every situation.

Following the idea of spreading Christianity in the same way that an infectious disease is spread, friends will not become Christians if their only contact is every two to three months (unless of course they are already seeking and then they will pursue you, rather than you needing to build relationship with them). Christians need to be seriously infected with the Jesus virus and then have maximum exposure to their friends. Interest groups are one way of increasing this exposure.

The story of an interest group for women by Liz West (April 2002)

"How do you help a group of women to develop a lifestyle of evangelism? Four years ago my cell of six women meeting on a midweek morning decided that we would run an Alpha-type course. We had been meeting socially with each others' friends over a period of months. It was not difficult to invite those friends, who seemed more interested in finding out about Christianity, to a lunch where we explained what we were going to do. Five friends said they would like to join the course. Each week we provided lunch and child care and by the end of the twelve weeks three of the women had become Christians.

These women were quickly assimilated into the cell, where they continued to grow in their understanding of God. Right from the beginning of their new life they became involved in reaching out to their friends. This was modelled to them as a normal part of being a Christian. Nine months later they invited nine of their friends to join a parenting course, using Care for the Family's Parent Talk material. This interest group was run by the cell over eight weeks and went so well that all the women wanted to continue the group and were prepared to talk about their beliefs and values. We continued to run the cell week by week during term time and opened up the group to our friends at various times to look at a series of relevant issues such as 'Love Languages', 'Making good relationships' or 'Personality types'. A year after the original parenting course these friends agreed to sign up to a series of mornings on what Christianity is all about. From this our cell grew to fourteen women, not all Christians, but all prepared to commit to a weekly meeting where we looked at the Bible and prayed for each other and for our unbelieving husbands and children, relatives and friends.

The cell began reaching out to another group of friends via another interest group. Twenty-one of us met fortnightly to cover issues around parenting teenagers. At the same time another cell which meets in the evening was getting to know the husbands of these women through parties and family outings. This led to two evenings on fathering and two more on post-modernism as experienced in parenting and in the work place.

Our daytime women's cell has now multiplied into two groups. We meet together about once a month for teaching, as the women are unable to make our Sunday gatherings because of family commitments. Some of these women have made commitments to the Lord, others are aware that they are on a journey. But all are involved with the cell community and make their contribution through the 4Ws meeting, praying and speaking out their thanks to God.

Over these four years we have seen a group of ordinary Christian women begin to reach a people group – young families in our town. The week by week prayers for these friends in the cell meeting are being answered. It has taken much longer than we thought, but the hearts of the Christians have been changed to love the lost in some way, as Jesus modelled to us. They use their time and money to make friendships at a level where they can be real and share their own story of what God is doing in their lives. They then work together to see these friends become Christians and be added to the cell. The group has developed new leaders and is ready for more growth. The goal of every cell member being involved in relational evangelism is being realised and each one is praying, believing for and working towards their part of the 'white harvest'."

Develop a share group

This is another idea developed by Ralph Neighbour and can be used when your cell has no obvious shared interest. A share group is set up, not on the basis of common interest, but on the basis of sharing the special interest of each member. So, for example, some members of the cell invite a few friends to a series of social meetings where the focus is around each person's special interest. One member is keen on Chinese cooking and creates a meal for the rest. On another evening another member talks about a trip they have taken to see the rain forests of South America. Another member has a musical interest which they share with the group. In this way the group meets in different homes, the host shares their special interest and the community is developed. Everyone enjoys sharing their experience or passion and Christians and non-Christians can contribute alike. Once the group has formed it is possible to introduce some Christian content.

Interest groups and cell meetings

Sometimes the entire cell will run an interest group. It is helpful to spread the sessions so that the members can meet in between for a regular cell meeting. It is often not realistic for Christians to give two nights a week for both cell and interest group meetings. Many cells decide to meet fortnightly during the life of an interest group and use the other week for their outreach via the interest group.

If only a few members of the cell are actually running the interest group then the rest of the group can meet to pray for the interest group while it is happening, either in the same home or at another venue.

Step 5 Witness outlines

Witness 1

Ask the group to discuss ideas for an interest group. Which skills or interests do members have which could form the focus of an interest group?

Some Interest group ideas:

- Gather a team that plays darts or skittles;
- A friend who is a brilliant golf player offers to give some group lessons;
- Use Colour Me Beautiful, a secular colour programme where a group of women can come together over four sessions to discover their colour and style;
- Wine tasting with teaching about different kinds of wine;
- A parenting course.

Witness 2

Challenge your cell to try to set up an interest group within the next six months.
What will it focus around and who will be invited?
What steps do you have to take with your friends in order for them to be prepared to join your interest group? (Do they need to meet the cell through a social activity? Does their Christian friend need to spend time with them socially before inviting them to the interest group?)
Devise a plan so that the cell, or some of it, will end up spending several sessions with five or six non-Christian friends around a focal interest, within the next six months.
Commit your plans to the Lord together.

Witness 3

Review your plans for the interest group on a regular basis and hold cell members accountable to pray for people contacted and for any social occasions in the run up to the interest group starting. During the course of the interest group there should be increased prayer activity.

Witness 4

It is important to begin to think what is the next step beyond the interest group. Relationships will have deepened, but are the friends ready to explore the Christian faith? Work out what is the next step for these friends and what the cell now needs to do to keep developing the relationships.

STEP 6 Content of the gospel

Goal: to create opportunities for our friends to hear the full gospel message.

Perhaps the hardest challenge for us at this time is seeing people moving from being open to the messenger to being open to the message. The hardest faith challenge is believing that people will become open to wanting to know the truth about Christianity. Once they are asking questions or open to learning about the truth we are generally more confident to explain what it means to be a Christian. Remember that most people need to hear the gospel several times in several different ways before they are ready to make any decision about accepting it as truth.

There are generally three situations in which people can hear the gospel and we need to be ready to create and use these different options. Individuals need to be equipped to share the gospel in one-to-one situations. Groups need to work together to create opportunities for explaining the gospel. Also, there are still occasions when taking someone to hear an evangelist present the gospel is a helpful step on an individual's journey.

It is helpful if your cell church has an Equipping Track in place which includes training in how to be a witness. This could include understanding the principles of Sowing Reaping and Keeping, plus a practical course such as Contagious Christianity from Willow Creek. We need to be trained in how to talk about the gospel in a relaxed and 'non-preachy' way.
See the Appendix *Equipped to Evangelise* starting on page 56.

Step 6 Witness outlines

Witness 1

Look at the most frequently asked questions about Christianity and make sure the whole cell knows how to answer these questions by working together as a group to create the answers. You could even produce a typed sheet of answers if it would help your members to have confidence, should the situation arise.

For example:
If God is a God of love, why is there suffering in the world?
Is the Bible true and authentic?
What happens to people of other faiths?
Why do Christians condemn gay people?
Why is church so boring?
What does it mean to be a Christian?

Suggested sources for these answers:
Letters from a Sceptic, by Gregory and Edward Boyd
Material from Alpha, by Nicky Gumbel

Witness 2

As we pray for people, the Holy Spirit will be seeking to bring them to a place of openness to the content of the gospel. Make a list of all the people in the cell community who do not know Jesus but whom you sense are nearing the point where they could hear the message. Ask the Holy Spirit to work in their lives so that they will become open to hearing it.

Witness 3

Get into pairs and practice telling your story, in three minutes, of how you came to faith and what has happened since.
Pray for opportunities to tell your story.

Witness 4

Discuss ideas for other ways of sharing the content of the gospel with your friends and pray for opportunities to do so.
For example, look for opportunities to give people a book to read with some Christian content, eg *The Testament*, by John Grisham, in which the hero becomes a Christian; and Jonathan Aitkin's autobiography, which describes his fall from cabinet minister and how he became a Christian.

Witness 5

Think of opportunities which your church as a whole could organise which would be of help to your friends on their spiritual journey; eg: Christmas and Easter programmes; social occasions to hear a celebrity giving their testimony; Bible weeks where you can go as a wider community with your non-believing friends who are ready for the content. You could ask your church leadership to organise one such event if several of your friends are ready to hear the message.

STEP 7 Create opportunities for your friends to become Christians

Goal: to plan opportunities for your friends to become Christians.

At the beginning of this booklet we gave a challenge for us to have confidence that the gospel is the best thing for our friends. To know Jesus is to have real life. If it is, then at the right point and the right time, we need to give our friends an opportunity to respond. Currently, because of the success of the Alpha course, this is a great deal easier than it has been in the past.

Planning an Alpha course

Cell-based Alpha

An Alpha course will not happen unless the cell team is working well. There will be those who have the relationships with friends who are ready for an Alpha course. Others will be radically praying. Others will have a home big enough to hold the course. Yet others will be needed to cook and teach and be there for relationship once the course gets going. The Alpha videos can be used, but it is also good to encourage cell members to do some teaching. This enables interactive questions throughout the whole session and has produced great results.

It is a fantastic tool for cells. When Alpha is run by a cell the whole group owns the evangelism process and as a result this is our preferred setting for the course. The seekers are welcomed into a quality Christian community in order to do the course. They will then find the transition into the cell an achievable next step for them. There is very little post-Alpha fall out as people who have appreciated the course find it easy to continue in that community. It overcomes the problem of how Alpha graduates go on to relate to the Church.

In a cell setting the Welcome questions can relate to the topic which is going to be discussed. The talk can even be given in the informal atmosphere around the meal table. If individuals have responded at the Holy Spirit weekend it can be helpful to begin the equipping materials straight after that as this encourages on-going connection between those individuals and the group.

As with interest groups it can be helpful to arrange Alpha on a fort-nightly basis, allowing the cell to meet in the intervening week. Many non-Christians find a bi-weekly meeting more achievable. This also gives more time for the community to form and deepen. What is lost is the intensity of the Alpha experience and the course can seem to go on for a very long time if it is over 24 weeks.

It is helpful to set the date for the Alpha course well in advance which provides an opportunity for cell members to focus on the relationships with those who may be ready to do the course. This will also provide a focus for the group and help it to move forward towards this goal.

Church-based Alpha

In other settings all the cell members with friends who are ready for Alpha can invite them to a centrally-run Alpha course. The work of preparing the meal is shared throughout the church and the teaching can be done by experienced speakers.

It is helpful if a cell picks up the challenge of hosting a table for the meal and leading a small discussion group so that once again the seeker is already involved in a cell community while doing the course.
Central Alpha courses usually have to run as an extra commitment in addition to cell life.

Whether the Alpha is run centrally or in a home, the Holy Spirit weekend seems to be the time when people make a commitment to Christ. It is helpful if the group can go away for this as it creates the intensity and faith challenge.

Other courses and opportunities
There are other courses available to use in a cell. For example the Emmaus course or the Why? course.
Event-based evangelism can be a useful time to bring a friend to the point of making a decision. In our current culture, non-Christians will probably only go to an event if they are at that point. Attending 'missions' does not have a good press in the non-Christian world. The difficulty, of course, is to hold the event at a time when various friends are at the point of making a decision.

Step 7 Witness outlines

Witness 1

Spend time together discussing when it would be appropriate to run a 'reaping' event such as an Alpha course. Pray for faith to believe that the cell will have enough people for such a course and then make plans to run it. Judging the timing of this can be difficult, but following an interest or share group could be a good time, or far enough in advance for the cell members to spend time socially with their friends. The goal is that relationships will be sufficiently deep with these friends that the risk of inviting them will not break the relationship. The bridge has to be strong enough to bear the load.
Arranging an Alpha course is always a risk and will require faith. It will focus the cell's efforts. If the date is not booked, the course will not happen! It is not helpful to wait till enough people are ready. Take a faith challenge, decide on a date and then plan what has to happen to get people ready for such an opportunity. Encourage the group to go for it!

Witness 2

Use the Witness section to make plans for the course or event. Hand out the jobs. Pray for each other and the friends who are invited. Keep each other accountable to do what is necessary to make it happen.

STEP 8 Growing the cell with new Christians

Goal: to prepare the cell to receive new or not-yet Christians.

Multiplying a cell

Cells multiply at different rates. Currently it takes about two to three years for a cell to work through all the steps, especially if the cell members begin with few non-Christian friends. Towards the end of the second year, it is good to plan a major initiative to invite the 'open' people in the network of friends to take a closer look at Jesus.

Much earlier than that though, some people might have become open to knowing more and would be willing to visit the cell. They need to be showing some genuine interest and to have become part of the cell community so that when they come to the cell meeting they already know the cell members. Experience says that this will be the exception and not the rule. Cell evangelism is not dragging people into a cell meeting, but it is empowering Christians to build true community. However, there may be the occasional person who would really like to know what happens in a cell meeting, so invite them in. Run the meeting as normal, explaining at the beginning what will be happening. Some non-Christians will love it. Part of my own conversion process was being invited into an open prayer meeting where people sat in a circle, and prayed one after another. I wasn't a Christian and knew little about Christianity, but I happily joined in the prayer meeting, and prayed when it was my turn.

Multiplying a cell around an interest group or Alpha course

One way of multiplying a cell could look more like cell planting. A team from the cell, which includes the new cell leaders, plants a new cell by holding an interest group or an Alpha course. The rest of the cell support this initiative, but instead of new people then coming back into the original cell, they continue on into a new cell community, creating two cells from the original one. The new cell leaders will lead a time of transitioning the Alpha course into a cell, by visiting the values base and purpose of a cell. They will then work with the new cell to create a new vision statement for it. Meanwhile the original cell gets on with reforming as a smaller group and reaching out to their friends who were not ready for the Alpha course, by whatever it takes to build the outer community as in Steps 4 and 5.

Step 8 Witness outlines

Witness 1

If you have a non-Christian visiting your cell:
Pray for the needs of non-Christians to be met by God, rather than for people to become Christians, which they would probably find offensive. Ask them to join in and share a need that they have or that a friend or family member of theirs might have.

Witness 2

If you have new Christians in your cell:
Start again from Step 1, changing the value to that of loving the lost, and then work through all the Steps again. Usually with new Christians in the group they have non-Christian friends in abundance and the cell can move through the steps very fast. In fact it is sometimes helpful to plan the next Alpha course very soon after the first one, just to accommodate the friends of the new believers. It is hoped that the momentum in reaching out will continue and new believers will always have an evangelistic life-style as a natural part of their Christian life.

Keeping the momentum going

The goal is to develop a lifestyle of relational evangelism in the cell. We are not looking for all-out activity, followed by months or maybe even years of doing nothing. Keep the momentum going by:

⇒ Working creatively on the Witness section;
⇒ Expecting God to answer your prayers;
⇒ Remembering to give God lots of praise when
⇒ prayers are answered;
⇒ Giving time for encouraging stories from cell members;
⇒ Giving leadership to the strategies for building relationships with the whole fishing team and their friends;
⇒ Modelling relational evangelism yourself as cell leader or supervisor;
⇒ Evaluating the progress of the cell community regularly with the cell members;
⇒ Regularly reviewing the goals of the cell with its members;
⇒ Encouraging members to be trained in evangelism and regularly reviewing this training;
⇒ Challenging negative attitudes to the lost;
⇒ Taking responsibility for each others' friends.

Finally . . .
Cell evangelism is all about hospitality, about building relationships and about loving and caring for people. Look at this fantastic letter written in the 2nd century AD by Aristides that shows how they did it and how, through their love and hospitality, they changed the Roman empire:

"Christians bear the divine laws impressed on their hearts and observe them in the hope of a future life. For this reason they do not commit adultery, or fornication; don't bear false witness; don't misappropriate the money they have received on deposit; don't

crave for what is not due to them; honour father and mother; do good to their neighbour; and when they are appointed judges, judge rightly.

They help those who offend them, making friends of them; do good to their enemies. They don't adore idols; they are kind, good, modest, sincere, they love one another; don't despise widows; protect the orphans; those who have much give without grumbling to those in need. When they meet strangers, they invite them to their homes with joy, for they recognise them as true brothers, not natural but spiritual.

When a poor man dies, if they become aware, they contribute according to their means for his funeral; if they come to know that some people are persecuted or sent to prison or condemned for the sake of Christ's name, they put their alms together and send them to those in need. If they can do it, they try to obtain their release. When a slave or a beggar is in need of help, they fast two or three days and give him the food they had prepared for themselves, because they think that he too should be joyful, as he has been called to be joyful like themselves.

They strictly observe the commandments of the Lord, by living in a saintly and right way, as the Lord God has prescribed to them; they give Him thanks each morning and evening for all food and drink and every other thing."

Excerpt taken from *Beyond the Clouds* by Laurence Singlehurst

Appendix

Equipped to evangelise

Introduction

In Ephesians 4:11-13 leaders are given the task of preparing their people for the works of ministry. As a result of this mandate, within the cell model there is an equipping track which is designed to prepare every Christian to be able to minister in different ways. Within this we would suggest that every cell member needs to be equipped in relational evangelism. The experience of cell life will help cell members to become motivated to reach out and will provide opportunities for working as a team. However, it will not train them to become witnesses. This training is the responsibility of church leadership and should be available to all church members as a separate course run over several weeks or at an equipping weekend.

We suggest that the curriculum for equipping cell members in relational evangelism includes the following modules:

Module 1 Understanding evangelism

- What should be our motivation for evangelism?
- Establishing thinking about what evangelism is – the process of sowing, reaping and keeping;
- Understanding the process of evangelism in our present culture;
- Understanding relational evangelism;
- The difference between 'rod' evangelism and 'net' evangelism.

Overcoming obstacles :

1 Unhelpful concepts of evangelism for our present culture;

2 Past experiences that have been painful or unfruitful which hold back the individual from engaging with non-Christians around faith issues.

Module 2 Working with gifts

- Learning to do evangelism your way – see styles of evangelism from Contagious Christianity, by the Willow Creek Organisation;
- What can you contribute? Knowing the gifts, strengths and resources available to each individual Christian which we can use in evangelism so that we can work from our strengths;
- Practical equipping in using spiritual gifts with non-Christians;
- Learning to pray with non-Christians.

Overcoming obstacles:

1 Breaking our stereotypes of the evangelist;

2 Helping each individual to know their unique contribution to seeing others become Christians;

3 Building confidence so that individuals can get started in evangelism.

Module 3 Building relationships from scratch

- Jesus' strategy for sending out the disciples to meet new people in Luke 10:5 -9;
- From acquaintance to friendship – developing friendships to the place where needs are shared and people are open to Christians so that they will become open to their message;
- How to make friends by having good inter-personal skills and being hospitable.

Overcoming obstacles:

1 Christians who have no friendships with people outside the Church;

2 Helping Christians to be able to develop friendships beyond the acquaintance stage;

3 Building confidence in those who do not consider themselves socially adept.

Module 4 Your story

- Learning to tell your story of how God met with you and what has happened since;
- Transitioning conversations in order to be able to witness to your own journey with God.

His story

- Knowing the full gospel and being able to talk about it in a way that will be relevant to those around you;
- Helping someone become a Christian - leading people to the point of making a decision.

Overcoming obstacles:

1 Building confidence in Christians to enable them to be witnesses and to lead someone to make a decision.

Module 5 The power of the net

- Building the community which includes Christians and non-Christians;
- Using the community to see people become Christians – developing 'interest' groups;
- Building an evangelism strategy – working strategically as a cell community to move people along the Engels scale;
- Running an Alpha course as a cell group.

Overcoming obstacles:

1 Cell members who do not take responsibility for the non-Christian contacts of other cell members;

2 Cells that are not seeing friends become Christians because they do not work together strategically;

3 Building a 'we can do this' atmosphere in the cell.

Other resources

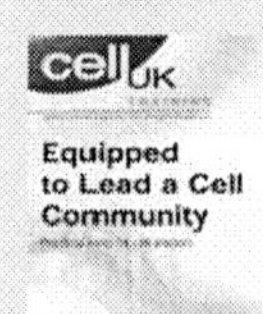

Equipped to lead a Cell Community
by Liz West and Trevor Withers
A great deal is learnt about how to lead a cell by observing a cell leader doing the job. What is not obvious is the thinking behind why cell life is arranged as it is and what unseen things are part of the task of cell leader. This book highlights these areas and brings some practical tools to enable potential leaders to understand the picture more fully. Whilst it will stand alone it can be used as a resource manual for those attending an Equipping Future Cell Leaders Course.

Equipping Future Cell Leaders
by Liz West and Trevor Withers with cell outlines by Jono West
This course has been designed to equip leaders to do more than lead a structured cell meeting. It is developed from the values base of the cell model and is an opportunity to establish the plumbline of cell for the new cell leaders.

Equipped to Supervise
by Liz West and Trevor Withers
Looking at the Cell Movement in the UK we have realised that supervision and coaching of cell leaders is essential. If a supervisor is not regularly visiting the cell and coaching the cell leader, the church leaders are working blind. Our new booklet, entitled Equipped to Supervise, gives an overview of the role of the cell coach and is full of practical insights. This booklet aims to help equip those who are supporting cell leaders.

Other resources

The Second Reformation
by William Beckham
Bill Beckham will walk you through the logic of a cell/ celebration structure from a biblical and historical perspective. His stories and illustrations make reading fun and bring the concepts to life. He provides you with a step-by-step strategy for launching your first cells. Many in the UK have proven that the thought-through principles and strategies given by Bill in this highly influential book work in practice.

Home Cell Group Explosion
by Joel Comiskey
Joel Comiskey traversed the globe to find out why certain churches and small groups are successful in reaching the lost. He found the answers and shares them in this thoroughly researched book. These pages are full of transferable principles that rekindle a vision for growth through evangelism and explain clearly key characteristics that determine evangelistic growth through a small group.

Redefining Revival
by *William Beckham*
At last! A book that is unafraid to look at the components that come together to stimulate and sustain revival while holding these in tension with God's sovereignty. Bill Beckham looks in his inimitable way at the context, roots and principles of revival and suggests strategies that will help us move towards a sustained growth situation in our churches. He clearly lays out biblical patterns for mission, evangelism and growth. The scope of his research and reflective thinking makes this a challenging and stimulating read.

Other resources

Sowing Reaping Keeping
by Laurence Singlehurst
Discover the reasons why evangelism may have been difficult in the past and learn new ideas to help you share your faith in a relevant way.

Loving the Lost
by Laurence Singlehurst
From his experience of working with numerous churches in the UK as they look at the cell church idea, Laurence Singlehurst explores the principles and practice of cell church. He works from basic definitions and values to practical application. A key focus is the area of evangelism through the cell church model.

8 habits of Effective Small Group Leaders
by Dave Earley
Discover the eight habits that will transform your cell group leadership. This is a real 'how to' book with plenty of application examples and guides. Good reading for those currently in cell group leadership or planning to take it on in the near future. A valuable resource for those supervising cells as they support and train leaders.

Easy ways to place your order:
phone: 02476 378599
e-mail: bookshop.kl@ywam.org.uk
Or for a full list of resources visit:
www.celluk.org.uk
Payment may be made by credit card or invoice.
Postage and packing will be charged extra.

About the authors

Laurence Singlehurst

A regular speaker at major events, such as Spring Harvest, and cell conferences worldwide, Laurence has also worked with numerous churches in the UK. However, his particular passion is equipping churches to reach their communities, with an emphasis on network evangelism, which is empowered by cell church structures.

Laurence dropped out of school in the early 1970s, and while travelling the world he was confronted with the love of Christ through members of the Jesus People movement, who subsequently led him to the Lord.

He is the author of *Evangelism Toolkit, Sowing Reaping Keeping, Loving the Lost* and *Beyond the Clouds*.

Liz West

Liz West works with Cell UK and is part of the leadership team of The Network Church in St. Albans which has been in cells for ten years. The opportunity to plant cell church has given her experience in leading and supervising cell groups through all the stages of cell life.

Leading a group of local church members through the process of changing values and structures has equipped her to help other leaders through written resources, conferences and consultations.